All My Relations

a prayer

Written and Illustrated
by

L. T. Sparrow

Arnold, California

L. T. Sparrow Publishing
P. O. Box 2675, Arnold, CA 95223
209-795-6311, Sparrowlt@aol.com

Published in the United States of America
Printed in Singapore by Star Standard Industries Pte. Ltd.

Dedicated
to
my children Lauri and Bryan
and their children's, children's, children.
My deepest gratitude to
my sister Marna, who lovingly holds my kite strings
and to all those friends and family whose love and
support have encircled me as this vision has been
birthed in book form.

Blessings to all.

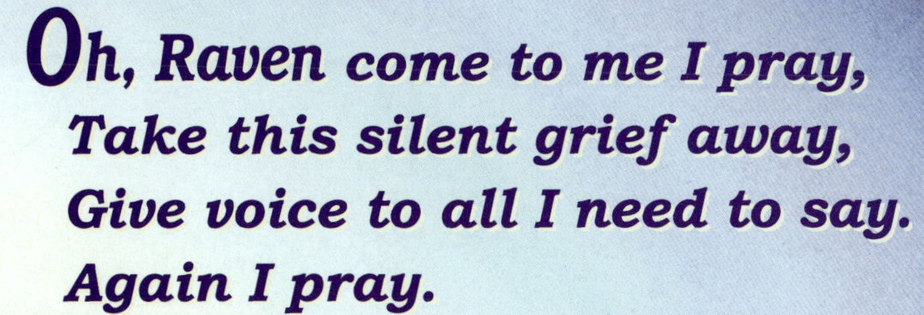

Oh, Raven come to me I pray,
Take this silent grief away,
Give voice to all I need to say.
Again I pray.

I walk the cracks between the worlds
And see beyond the veils unfurled
To endless possibilities
Of our yet unmanifest destiny.
Despair or love have equal chance
And so between the veils I dance.
Sometimes I cry, sometimes I wail,
Sometimes I laugh or sing all day
But most importantly I pray
That all of humankind will see
The beauty of equality
And drop their armor and their
swords
And hear beyond encultured
words.

My skin is light, my eyes are green
And so the native lies unseen
Beneath a skin that's soft and pale . . .

There lives a dark skinned warrior, male.
With arrows sheathed and bow in hand
He stands as guardian of the land.
His weapons now beseeching words,
He thinks perhaps they go unheard,
So sits in council everyday
And all relations come to pray.

Some lying prostrate on the earth,

Some kneeling begging for rebirth,

Some standing garbed
in heavy cloaks,

And others sitting making smoke.

Some chirp their cheerful
winged songs,

Or howl their message loud and long.

Some beat their tails upon the ground
And make the most alarming sound.

Some hold within their silent forms
The secrets of how earth was born,

And some with open branches stand,
A bridge between the sky and land.

Still others croak,

Some purr,

Some hiss,

There is no "greater than" or "less"
For every voice is equally heard,

Creepers,

Swimmers,

Animals,

Birds,

The standing stones,

The ancient trees,

What was,

What is,

And what will be?

Inhabitants from distant space
And humankind of every race,
Sisters, brothers, all are we
Rejoicing in equality.

My skin is light, my eyes are green
But many bloodlines through me stream
I cannot claim one tribe or race,
But see myself in every face.
So warrior put your heart at ease,

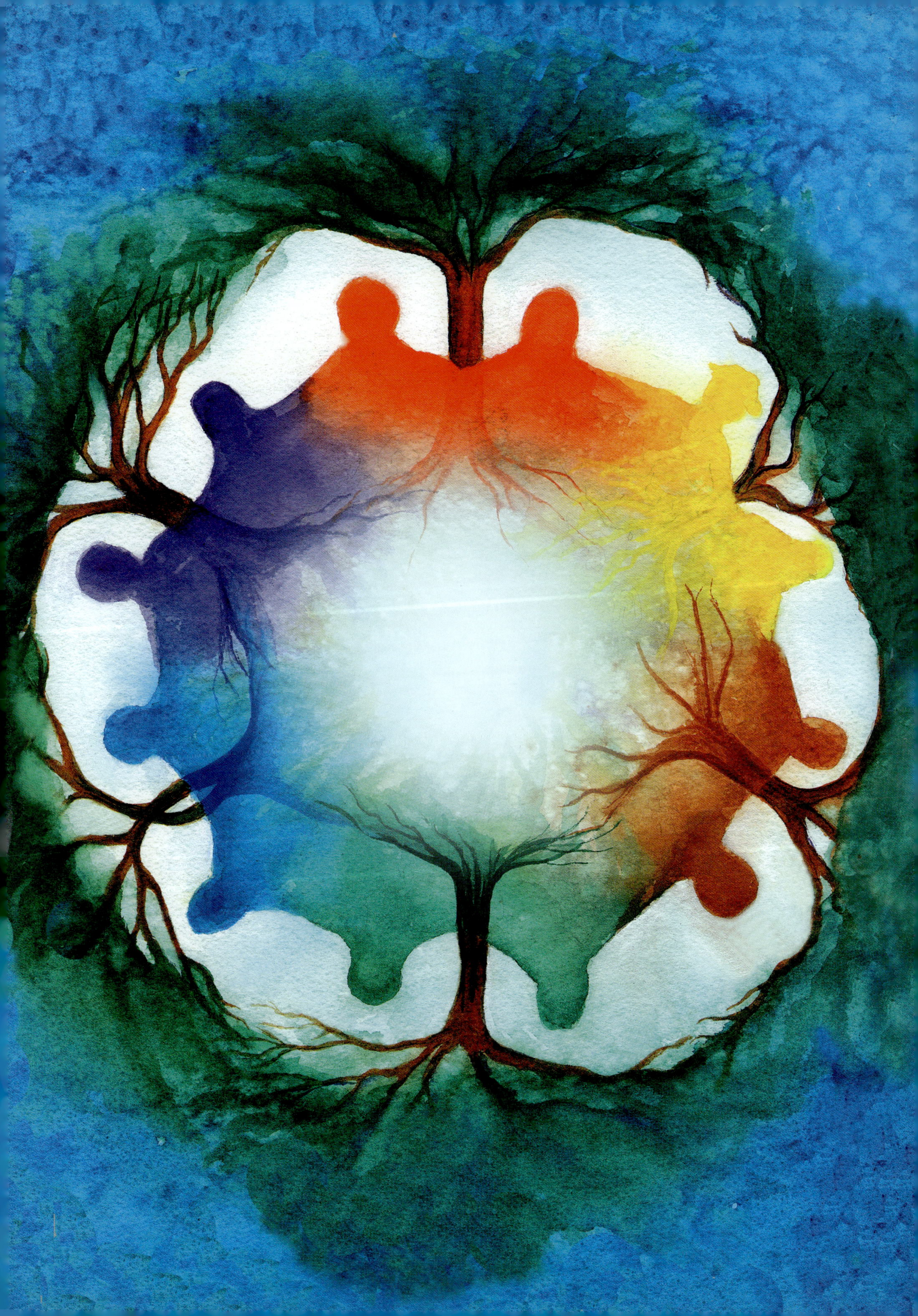

Ho Mitakuye Oyasin

This book is offered with the deepest respect for these teachings and for native people everywhere.

AUTHOR'S NOTES

The title of this book, *All My Relations*, comes from the Lakota words *Ho Mitakuye Oyasin*. The literal translation means "All My Relations," or "I am related to all things and all things are related to me." These words are spoken at the end of a prayer, or as an affirmation of a truth having been heard, much the same way "Amen" is used in Christianity.

These words, *Ho Mitakyue Oyasin,* also refer to the sacredness of all living things. When we pray, we pray with, and for, the whole of creation and with our Mother/Father Creator who goes by many, many names.

In some tribal traditions Raven is the trickster. In the context of this book, Raven is the messenger of the void and the bringer of healing.

In the beginning pages of this book, the storyteller and the warrior are each holding a flower from the medicinal creosote plant, one of the most ancient life forms on the planet. The warrior is a stylized version of Geronimo, the famous Chiricahua Apache war leader who fought hard to protect his family and his land. He has become known around the world, and he is used as a symbol of courage in the face of overwhelming odds in the fight for freedom and justice. Geronimo's image is also on the transparent page. He died a prisoner at Fort Sill, Oklahoma in 1909. *Photo courtesy Arizona Historical Society; 949 E Second Street, Tucson, Arizona 85719 [Accession #19689].*

The images in this book were chosen to represent endangered species and vanishing cultures from the six major continents. The following list specifically refers to the page, "and humankind of every race." It begins with the asterisk (*) located near the ladybird beetle at the top of the circle of insects and spirals outward in a clockwise direction.

1. Ladybird Beetle
2. Fungus Beetle
3. Grasshopper
4. Stag Beetle
5. Cicada
6. Scorpion
7. Copper Butterfly
8. Dragonfly
9. Spider
10. Praying Mantis
11. Ant
12. Long-horned Borer
13. Ladybird Beetle
14. Fluminense Swallowtail
15. Grasshopper
16. Stag Beetle
17. Cicada
18. Scorpion
19. Butterfly
20. Dragonfly
21. Queen Alexandra's Birdwing
22. Praying Mantis
23. Ant
24. Longhorned Borer
25. Diamondback Rattlesnake
26. Spotted Salamander
27. Olm Salamander
28. Spur-thighed Tortoise
29. Canebrake Rattlesnake
30. Pancake Tortoise
31. Lizard
32. Chaco Tortoise
33. Hochester Frog
34. Fijian Manatee
39. Common Sturgeon
40. Bowhead Whale
41. Nile Crocodile
42. Coelacanth
43. Pirarucu
44. Boto (fresh water dolphin)
45. Dugong
46. Giant clam
47. Baiji, (fresh water dolphin)
48. Mekong Catfish
49. Buffalo
50. Gray Wolf
51. Wildcat
52. Reindeer
53. African Elephant
54. Gorilla
55. Vicuna
56. Jaguar
57. Ring-tailed Wallaby
58. Koala
59. Tiger
60. Giant Panda
61. Native North American
62. Eskimo
63. Russian
64. Lapp
65. India, Bondo Woman
66. Arabian Bedouin
67. Native Bolivian
68. Native Bolivian
69. New Guinea Asmat Woman
70. New Guinea Asmat Man
71. Japanese Woman
72. Tibetan Man
73. Spotted Owl
74. Bald Eagle
75. Dalamatian Pelican
76. Red Kite
77. Hermit Ibis
78. Madagascar Fish Eagle
79. Hyacinth Macaw
80. Andean Condor
81. Ascension Frigatebird
82. Abbot's Booby
83. White-eyed River Martin
84. Siberian Crane
85. Giant Redwood
86. Oak
87. Acacia
88. Banyan
89. Eucalyptus
90. Cypress

* " The standing stones" Monument Valley, Stonehenge, the Pyramids, Easter Island, Ayers Rock Mount Kailas in Tibet.

ABOUT THE AUTHOR

L. T. "Sparrow," an innovative artist and poet, spent much of her childhood with her missionary parents in the Bolivian jungles. After returning to Los Angeles in the 1960s she pursued a bachelor of arts degree in religious studies and a master of arts degree from the University of San Francisco. She has traveled extensively in Asia and the Americas and has raised two children. These experiences have afforded her a unique world view, which she expresses through her art and life philosophy.

MANY OF THE IMAGES IN THIS BOOK ARE AVAILABLE AS CARDS AND PRINTS

For more information

L. T. Sparrow

P. O. Box 2675, Arnold, CA 95223

Sparrowlt@aol.com 209-795-6311